True Leadership

How to lead by serving others first

Jeffrey Ellis
10/2/2018

Acknowledgements

At "Biker Sunday" in August 2018, I walked over to Luke Barber, President of Barber Packaging Company, in Bangor, Michigan and said, "Hey Luke, what do you think about the leadership characteristics I sent over to you for my new book?" "Well," he said, "I read your list, and it sounds like, when you come right down to it, the most powerful leadership principles are already spelled out in First Corinthians 13." I stopped, stunned. "Wow, I think you're right." I walked away rubbing my head. Luke was right. The best leadership characteristics have been right in front of us the whole time. They are about loving others.

My son, David Ellis, also weighed in with his insights. Dave is an international entrepreneur who has been working and living in Africa for the past ten years. He started a poultry company in Ethiopia and has run it successfully, against overwhelming odds, for nearly a decade. I wanted to use Jesus as the best example of servant leadership, but I was concerned about how businesspeople would react. "Don't worry about using Jesus as your example. The business world knows who He is," He said smilingly. "If it's true, then it's true. Go with it." Dave was right, too. Jesus is the greatest leader of all time, and most of us know who He is.

My best friend, Bob Klein, and I learned of servant leadership and put it into practice (though not perfectly) in the late 1990s. He is a graduate of West Point and had been an officer in the special forces of the United States

Army for seventeen years. So, he already knew many of the principles. Even though our career paths have separated us, we continue to embrace these ideals as fundamentals of servant leadership.

Author's Note

My study of servant leadership began in 1995 after I became a Christian. While some of the principles of *True Leadership* are biblically based, I also understand that many people are not believers. *True Leadership* and the principles of servant leadership are for everyone, regardless of their faith. My goal was to identify universal principles that we can all use to serve others and become better leaders.

If you are interested in what I believe and the inspiration for my personal and professional pursuits, please read *The Highest Standard* at the back of the book or visit me at: www.jeffellis.us.

Introduction

Are there leadership principles that we can learn from servant leaders of the past? If so, what are they? The corporate world is swamped with lousy leadership. Companies are crippled with self-serving, arrogant, prideful "leaders." Company offices are choked with petty tyrants and bureaucrats instead of servants. True leadership is so much more than the answer to the question, "Who's in charge?"

The idea of servant leadership is so explosive, so contrary to established principles, so antagonistic to the prevailing culture, that I wonder if it can be understood, absorbed, or appreciated. I fully expect that some will nod in agreement with servant leadership principles, but they won't change. Nonetheless, some might. Somewhere, someone is aching to be better than they are. Someone is out there who cares deeply about those in his care.

Let's be crystal clear about this. There are some who claim to be servant leaders. They loudly make their claims and sell their books. But, as former British Prime Minister Margaret Thatcher said about being a lady, "If you have to tell people you are one, you probably aren't." Servant leaders don't seek the spotlight, don't chase the bestselling lists, and sacrifice themselves for the sake of others. It is a quiet, humble undertaking to die to yourself every day. But the rewards are powerful and eternal. Everything becomes possible for those who believe.

Businessmen, scholars, and authors have been searching for the essential qualities of leadership for decades. Who would have thought they were right in front of us all the time? That they are the timeless characteristics of love?

What would happen if these ancient leadership principles were implemented in the workplace? What kind of teams could we build? How could we change the world? What success, progress, and profitable work could we enjoy? As leaders, we can do more than imagine—we can change. And change we must, if we are to truly lead.

Table of Contents

"He who is greatest among you shall be your servant."

—Jesus

Chapter One
Leadership

The world, in all its realms, is desperate for leaders. There is especially need for leaders who seek peace and can reconcile factions. There is a growing cry for leadership that acts in humility, respect, and civility. From families to government, we seem to be a nation starved for leadership that considers others' interests more than its self-interests. Servant leadership satisfies that hunger.

Everyone has the potential to be a leader. That doesn't mean everyone wants to be or will be a leader, but the potential is there. The ability to meet that challenge resides in every one of us. Some leaders are more naturally gifted than others, but great leadership can be learned. How? Because we can all learn how to serve others.

Unfortunately, the idea of what it means to be a leader is largely misunderstood. Much of our management class in America has become a caricature of true leadership. The modern understanding of leadership tends toward the self-serving, the arrogant, or the blustering manager. To many, it means "the one who is in charge," or the boss. But the essential understanding for all people in leadership is that they are servants before they are bosses. People who are out to prove something, who are dominating and controlling, will always exercise their responsibilities badly.

We are so inclined to want leadership for the prestige, honor, and applause that comes with it. "Inside each of us is a little tyrant who wants power" and to control everything. We tend to "interfere in the work of others, taking charge, jealously guarding our authority." Our tendency is to allow freedom for others only when it doesn't conflict with our ideas and when we can control it. This is a trap. Dr. L. Morrill Burke at the University of Southern Maine taught, "The nature of evil is the impulse to power over others." The desire to control is, at its core, dangerous and destructive. Leaders must resist that temptation and erect ramparts of freedom around the group they are leading to buttress that inclination.

The greatest leaders are those who are the greatest servants. The scriptures teach us that "the chief of all will be the greatest servant of all." The servant leader truly knows he is responsible, primarily, for others. Everything else flows from that understanding. He acts for their benefit, makes decisions for their good, and puts their needs above his own. Leadership is to "help the growth and freedom of individuals." Serving others is an act of love. To sum it up, true leadership is about loving other people.

This is easier said than done. There is plenty of strife and potential conflict in the workplace. But the servant leader insists on considering other peoples' needs before his own. The leader is the guardian of unity. His mission is to create an atmosphere of mutual trust, confidence, sharing, and peace within the team. "Human beings grow best in a relaxed environment built on mutual confidence." He does not fear conflict. He accepts it and strives to be an instrument of reconciliation. Every leader has the task of peace and reconciliation.

Servant leadership always puts the needs of the group and the team above its own. Most people want to know, "Does he care about me?" The servant leader answers that question: "More than anything." When people see that, they rally to the cause, delivering more of themselves than they would otherwise. To be a part of a team that cares about the individual stimulates the very best efforts of the individual contributor.

There is no perfect leader who has every leadership gift in sufficient measure. And he should not be afraid to admit that. He ought to be humble enough to ask for support. There is a tendency, even among servant leaders, to believe that everything the team needs depends on him or her alone. It ain't so. The wonder and beauty of great teams is that they can nurture and even heal themselves. The leader who has invested himself in the team can find a rich and ready source of help and restoration. The same grace with which he leads can be found in equal measure in the group itself. Being human is not a character flaw. And needing healing is not failing. It can be a powerful by-product of a well-led team.

Imagine a world-class sled team. The lead dog is in the harness, along with the rest of team, eager to get underway. The leader isn't the driver with the whip. The true leader is the lead dog, setting the pace, driving himself harder than the rest, pulling more than his weight, doing more than his share. He sets the example, throwing himself into the task, as an example to others to show he is taking care of the team. Should he stumble, the others take up the slack. They pull their share and his, too. Humans are more complex than sled dogs, but the illustration is about the dynamic.

In 1999, my friend, Bob Klein, and I were responsible for a large sales team that sold more than $1B in securities. We were just learning the tenets of servant leadership and quickly discovered we had a lot to learn. We believed that there were only two reasons why anyone failed. Either we hired the wrong person, or we didn't support them enough. Both of those responsibilities were ours. Our job was to support every producer and clear obstacles out of their way. If a new hire didn't work out, the fault was ours, not theirs.

The core principle of servant leadership is to consider others before oneself. This concept stands conventional management theory on its head. True leaders give all the credit to the team and take all the blame when things go wrong. This is not a system that rewards the arrogant and the self-serving. But it is a system that honors and respects those who honor and respect others.

True leaders look at an impossible situation and say, "We can do this. We've got this." How? Because they know it doesn't depend on them alone. Without regard for self but with eyes wide open to the potential of others, this team can do the impossible. How? They are empowered by principles deeper than the status quo. They are energized by the most unstoppable, long-suffering, patient, and unfailing power the world has ever known: love.

It will seem irrelevant to some, corny to others, and too emotional for many. But love is not primarily a romantic feeling—it is an action. More than that, it is an action that places others above oneself. The power of love has been driving human behavior since the beginning of time. And it has lost none of its potency. As long as people are dealing with people, it is relevant. And just because the concept is ancient doesn't mean it's not still relevant.

But many of us have lost the understanding of true love and what it means for leadership. We have wrapped it up in feelings and romance. While both of those can be found in relationship, that is not the nature of love. The nature of love is self-sacrifice for the benefit of another. Therein lies the power, beauty, and heart of leadership and love.

Serving others does not appeal to one's pride as much as applause and glory do. It is a quiet, selfless work. But deep within it lies satisfaction, peace, and a sense of well-being. There is a joy that comes from knowing that the team did something no single person could have done alone. And no single person should receive the credit. Leadership always defers the credit and the glory to the team.

There is something profound that occurs in the soul of a leader when others succeed. There is a satisfaction and grace that is released only by stepping back from the stage and letting the team have the spotlight and applause. The greatest pleasure I have known in business is to see people I have served serve others. Some have become national leaders in large companies, and others are sole practitioners flourishing in their professions. I rejoice in their success as if it were my own.

Strong leaders surround themselves with strong leaders. The reverse is also true. Weak leaders tend to surround themselves with weak leaders. One of the secrets of servant leadership is to be constantly looking for servant leaders to promote. The leader seeks to replicate himself with someone who will also care for the team. Taken to its logical conclusion, true leadership has the consequence of helping others succeed. In this way, the legacy cascades down through the generations.

Caveat

We all look for perfect leaders with wisdom, insight, and compassion. Then, we become disappointed when their humanity shows up. They fall short of our expectations. There is a measure of grace that needs to be given to leaders. They will fail, sooner or later. They have their limitations and failings like everyone else. There needs to be opportunity for redemption for them. We are not children. Everyone makes mistakes. A good team will restore its leadership and extend grace for recovery. Nobody's perfect.

Chapter Two
Servant Leadership

Modern leadership theory places the CEO at the top of the corporate structure. This command-and-control model was borrowed from the military because it had served well during WWI and WWII. But in civilian business and industry, it is flawed. The general's goal is victory. The factory manager's goal is profit. But the servant leader's goal is the growth of individuals in love and truth. That model puts the customer and those who deal with the customer at the very bottom of the hierarchy. In fact, the top leaders are the ones furthest removed from the ones who matters most up and down the organization.

Servant leadership posits the reverse. The most important business activity is to serve others. And the chief officer, the "C-level executive's" role is to provide resources and remove obstacles to those closest to the customer. Most corporations have this spectacularly wrong and have paid the price or will pay the price. How? The modern marketplace is an amazing leveling force.

How then do you change the world without a suite of senior executives in corner offices? Simple. You get a new focus. Smash the org structure. Turn the pyramid of corporate culture upside down. Loudly, clearly, and passionately declare that the mission of the company is to serve others. Invert the organizational triangle, and make the customer the most important person and the chief executive the least. In fact, his position at the bottom of the org chart deliberately shows that his or her role is to support and serve the entire organization. And the closer we are to the customer, the more important we are to the enterprise.

How then shall we lead?

To quote Pastor Bill Johnson of Bethel Church in Redding, California, we are called to "lead with the heart of a servant and serve with the heart of a king." There is something so special and so powerful in humility that it escapes the notice of many people. The civility, compassion, and winsomeness of a humble servant leader unlocks the best in others. A great CEO leader with the heart of a servant will be highly valued, regardless of where his name is on the org chart.

Seven Essential Characteristics of Leadership

I searched the available literature and scoured my experiences to distill the essential elements of servant leadership into this book. In the end, I found them in an unexpected place: the Bible. It was like finding buried treasure. There is a famous passage that lists the very characteristics manifested by outstanding servant leaders. It is no accident that the characteristics of true leadership are, in fact, the same as the characteristics of love. This is what it says:

> *"Love is patient, love is kind. It does not envy, it does not boast, it is not proud. It does not dishonor others, it is not self-seeking, it is not easily angered, it keeps no record of wrongs. Love does not delight in evil but rejoices with the truth. It always protects, always trusts, always hopes, always perseveres. Love never fails."*

Chapter Three
Love is patient.

Leadership is patient. It endures difficulties, frustrations, and setbacks. The root word for "patience" is the Greek term makrothumia, meaning longsuffering and forbearance. It is like a "candle with a very long wick." In the face of difficulty and misunderstanding, patience refuses to give up on someone. True leadership long-suffers people who are difficult to work with. Far too often and far too easily, we get exasperated and give up on people too soon.

Patience is not tapping our toes, waiting for others to finally "get it." Leaders do not have a "monopoly on insights and gifts; their role, on the contrary, is to help everyone exercise their own gifts for the good of the whole." Patience is the essence of recognizing that there are insightful, creative, and wise people at work on a given problem, and it is not always up to the leader to diagnose and resolve every problem. Patience withholds her immediate response. She sometimes withholds the obvious solution or "quick fix" to allow for a better solution to emerge.

Practicing patience allows time for wisdom to be revealed. Patience resists the temptation to jump in and make all things right or solve every problem. It allows for an unraveling to occur as people become actively engaged in disentangling the mess. Patience exudes a quiet confidence in the ability of others. Patience says, "I will check my voice in favor of the wisdom of the group." It esteems others above itself.

We live in a world of instant gratification. As leaders, it is our responsibility to set the pace, to lead the tempo of the group. It is up to us to show great patience. We tend to be victims of the urgent rather than the important. We must discern the competing priorities and sort them out. The loudest problem isn't necessarily the most important issue on my to-do list. For problems that are not on fire, there is time for others to participate in the decision-making process. And we need to have patience to allow the team to do its job.

Impatience causes mistakes. The right answer, the best solution, can get buried under a flurry of hurried responses. Wisdom requires time to do her work. The subconscious mind, where the greatest speed and most powerful reasoning capacity reside, works in the background, not the foreground. That requires time.

Also, being first and foremost to resolve the crisis, the leader sets him or herself up for the next crisis. Always looking for an immediate resolution sets the expectation for the leader to *always fix everything*. That will not always be the best solution. In the dramatic in-flight rescue of Apollo 13, there was a leader in the space capsule on one end of the radio and the control tower on the other. He had to remain patient; he could not fix the situation himself. It took the whole team back in Houston to diagnose, problem-solve, and recommend a solution that would save the mission and the astronaut's life. What a powerful example of patience under pressure. The tyranny of the urgent must be held back to give time for the whole team to respond.

Most of the time, in the world of business, lives are not at risk. We have time to think and to engage the collaborative insights, experience, and collective brilliance of our group. How many disasters could have been averted if patience ruled and consultation and collaboration were employed?

Myers Briggs says I am an ENTJ. I tend to see problems and solutions visually. Not everyone processes the world the same way. I tend to be impatient. Sometimes, I clearly see the way, but other people want to study the alternatives. I am learning to trust those who process their sensory perceptions differently than I do. Practice is showing me that there is wisdom in a multitude of counsellors.

I am not a naturally patient person. My tendency is to check my inward witness, my gut intuition, to see if it makes sense. I don't tend to stop and solicit opinions on important issues. If I make decisions without the creativity and wisdom of the team, I have failed. But if I am patient and submit to the team, I overcome my single biggest obstacle to leading others: myself.

Being a leader means we are willing to draw from deep wells of patience and kindness.

Chapter Four
Love is kind.

To be kind means to be willing to serve the needs of others first. Kindness does not seek its own needs, reputation, or glory. It looks upon the needs of others and is willing to sacrifice for them. It acknowledges individual gifts, idiosyncrasies, and circumstances and respects them. Kindness goes out of its way to recognize others. It opens the door of opportunity or recognition and allows others to enter first. Kindness births courtesy and civility and benevolence. It is a learned behavior that grows in us through practice and patience.

There was a poor father, rattled by doubt and unbelief, who sought Jesus to help his son who was suffering from demonic torture. The desperate father confessed his lack of faith and broke down crying, saying, "Please help my unbelief [in you]." Instead of criticizing or rebuking him, Jesus responded with great kindness and immediately healed his son.

John Wooden was a kind, thoughtful, and gentle man. He was also the coach of the UCLA basketball team from 1948 to 1975. At the beginning of every season, he patiently taught each player how to carefully put on their socks to prevent blisters. He knew that if he cared for them and treated them with love and respect, they would feel better, practice harder, and perform better. He led UCLA to 10 national championships in 12 years. He coached some of the greatest stars of the game. He poured his life into those players, and they ended up loving him and working their hearts out for him and for each other. Nothing was impossible for them. His kindness and faith led them through every challenge, on and off the court.

"Duke" Chapman served as the Chairman and CEO of the Chicago Board of Options Exchange (CBOE) for 13 years. In the mid 90s, he was the Chairman of the Board of ABN Amro Financial Services in Chicago, Illinois, where I worked for him. Duke was the kindest and most gracious man I ever served. I was a sales manager for him during the infamous meltdown of the tech industry in 2000 to 2002. Even when the customers were panicky and the brokers were nervous, he was unflappable, unswerving, and steady. At one of my lowest points, I was in trouble and didn't know where to turn. I called Duke for advice. He dropped everything and said, "I'm sure two guys from Maine can figure something out. Let's get together." No matter how busy or pressed he was, he always took time for me. He was the epitome of grace under pressure. His grace and kindness have stayed with me through life. Duke was a world-class servant leader.

The common ingredient in each of these stories is the same: kindness. Often overlooked and rarely encouraged, it is a powerful leadership principle. Let me put it this way: it is so underdeveloped in today's culture that it will catch people off-guard.

Chapter Five
Love rejoices in the truth.

Leadership delights in the truth. It celebrates honesty and truth-telling. It deliberately seeks and publishes the truth, even when it's inconvenient or counter to the current cultural climate. Truthfulness examines itself first. It shines a spotlight on its own activities and says, "Examine me and see if there is anything that needs to be changed."

With certain people, there is a tendency to "spin" the story. Revealing some facts and downplaying others can be tantalizing for those sensitive to market pressures. As a leader and entrepreneur, I never wanted the facts to be distorted. I needed the bare truth. Only then could I understand what was really going on. Marketing executives may want to accentuate the positives, but a leader must insist on knowing and using the bare facts of the situation without varnish. It is only in this way that informed, thoughtful, honest decisions can be made. There is no room for mutual mystification for true leaders.

A leader doesn't distort the facts to make things sound better or reflect more favorably on himself. The truth stands alone, unvarnished and exposed. We are called upon to always use fair weights and measures. Integrity does not bow the knee before political correctness or "optics." We may lose business when we refuse to go along with the crowd, but we will win in the end with a reputation for honesty and fair dealing.

Jesus spoke the truth even at the cost of his personal reputation. He just didn't care about the praise of men. The Pharisees, the political power of His day, were always after Him to trip Him up. Despite their threats and traps, He always told them the truth, even when it cost Him everything. He saw through their self-aggrandizing actions and pretenses and called on them to do their jobs—to teach people according to the law, not according to their own self-serving interests. He stood firm in the truth and wouldn't back down or back off. The same courage is badly needed in today's conference rooms.

Those who rejoice in the truth are not easily shaken when an accusation rails against them. A person of integrity stands by truthfulness even when a decision is unpopular or costly. Honesty and straightforwardness must not be sacrificed on the altar of convenience or "correctness." We are to deal with people fairly and honestly at all time and in all ways. Everybody gets a fair shake.

Servant leaders rejoice in the truth. We reap what we sow. If we sow seeds of honesty, integrity, and truth, we will harvest the same. It is easy to go along with popular trends. It takes courage to stand against the crowd. But every sailor knows the optimum position of the sailboat is the beam reach, that point of sail where the wind blows across the boat, not behind it. The goal of every sailor is to position his boat and sails in the optimum position to achieve the best forward momentum. Optimal forward progress requires resistance.

If we are continually bandied about by the ever-changing winds of popular trends, we will always have an uncertain course. When Chik-fil-A was recently castigated by the popular press for an unpopular stand, they quietly stuck to their guns and watched as customers voted with their feet and their wallets. Instead of joining a boycott, millions stood in line at restaurants across the country in silent support of their beloved franchise. Recently, the political left tried to vilify In-N-Out burger for not supporting liberal causes. The backlash against the left was immediate. In-N-Out quietly continued doing what they do, and their defenders, including many liberal voices, came to their rescue. Steadfast belief in core principles and great hamburgers can withstand hysterical outrage. There are some things you just don't mess with.

And there are times when making a stand is the honest course of action. Martin Luther King did so on behalf of civil rights. Nelson Mandela took a stand for political equality in a divided country. Ronald Reagan and Margaret Thatcher stood against the power and evils of the former Soviet Union. In all these cases, public opinion bowed before their courageous stands. In America, such stands are not uncommon. They are the fruit of free speech and individual rights. If businesses are indeed corporate citizens (Citizens United), is there a calling on us, too, to stand for truth?

Risky business, that. Or so we think. Courageous business, at the least. Dare we take a public stand and risk offending our customers? Is it our place? Every organization needs to decide upon what hill, if any, they are willing to plant their flag and die. Very few will risk that. But public stands need not be political stands. Truth is truth. Accurate reporting, honest measures, and financial statements are all part of the truth package. Full and fair disclosure to consumers without deceit or manipulation are hills where flags should be planted. These are areas where truth must reign, even when it makes them unpopular with analysts and markets.

Chapter Six
Love always protects.

The Greek word used in this verse for "protects" is *stego*, which means to cover, like a roof covers a house. But it means so much more. The concept includes protecting, shielding, and guarding people from external threats. The leader, operating in love, is protective of his group. He shields them from distractions, guards them from unwarranted criticism, and covers them under his authority.

My daughter, Annie, lives on a farm with chickens. She recounted one day when a hawk was circling overhead. When the hawk's shadow passed over a group of young chicks, the mother hen cackled at the little ones, and they scurried under her wings. They nestled safely beneath her wings until the danger had passed.

Leaders protect people. They look especially for those whose personalities or dispositions make them vulnerable to attack. Leadership lifts her wings and covers those who are most vulnerable to attack or abuse. The tyranny of the majority can be a bully to the dissenter. Sometimes, that small voice is the inspired voice of solution and progress. Thuggery is checked by the strong hand of a leader.

There was a woman, famously caught committing adultery, who was thrown at Jesus' feet by the lawyers, demanding judgment. He agreed that the law provided judgment for such an offense and invited the lawyer without sin to cast the first stone. No one could answer that call. True character is exposed in how leaders treat someone who cannot advance their agenda. How does the leader treat someone seemingly insignificant to him or her? That interaction can reveal a great deal.

The isolation of leadership is widely quoted: "It's lonely at the top." It's even lonelier when the weight of the world lays upon the shoulders of the leader. It is in those times that the character of the true leader is revealed. True leaders never pass the buck; that weight of responsibility is theirs to bear. When things go badly, when everything goes wrong, leaders tell the world, "I'm to blame. That is my fault. I am responsible for that." And when things go right, the true leader points to the team and tells the world, "They did that! They deserve all the credit!" In the words of my friend and leader, Rich Hotham, I have never found a true leader who believes his or her own press clippings. Instead, he or she always uses success to celebrate the team's accomplishments.

Leaders empower everyone on the team. Every voice matters. If you have a leader who does not respect the sound of each voice, find a new team. Leaders protect dissenters. They make it "safe" to have an opinion that goes against the conventional. If there is criticism to be leveled, the leader takes the brunt. They protect the object of their affection, the team. That is the price of leadership.

True leaders always protect their teams.

Chapter Seven
Love always trusts.

A true leader looks for the best in others. Sometimes, this requires the leader to doubt his doubts, to push back in disbelief of what he sees and hears and feels. Trust says, "I believe in that person. I choose to accept the best in them. I will look for the best in them." Mark Batterson, lead pastor of National Community Church in Washington, D.C. uses this leadership principle with his staff. "We choose to look for the best in people, the best of the situation, and the best of their efforts, gifts, and talents. You can always find faults. But are you willing to always find the best in someone?"

The default position for the true leader is to trust. Sooner or later, someone may violate that trust, but until that day, everyone is presumed worthy. And when they are not, they are met with mercy instead of judgment, and grace is extended for them to recover from the fall. There should always be grace to fail. Failing to reach an objective is not, in itself, reason for discipline if that person acted in honesty and integrity. Failing to try at all is the deeper failure.

Sometimes, we must trust others in spite of themselves, even in spite of betrayal. In times like that, we need to speak into people's lives with words of confidence and kindness. It is in those very times, when they least deserve our trust, that we should restore them for the benefit of the team.

Simon Peter was unpredictable. Although he was a senior member of the team, he was up and down. One moment, he was emulating Jesus, walking on water, only to lose focus and nearly drown. When he was confronted by the rabble-rousers, he denied ever knowing Jesus, whom he lived with for three years. But Jesus always saw the best in Peter. He told Peter that he was solid as a rock, and He trusted him to carry on the work of the church long after He was gone. And he did. Peter became a bold voice and leader of the early church. Peter became outspoken, courageous, and dependable. He became a servant leader of the church.

The Micro-Manager

The management personality that operates without any trust in the team is the micro-manager. He involves himself in every decision and never allows people to do their jobs. When he second-guesses everything, he is really saying, "I don't trust you." Unfortunately, this type of manager is far too common in today's business world.

Micro-managers look to impose themselves on every decision, tying the hands of those to whom they have given responsibilities. People have a right to make their own mistakes and fall on their faces. Those who power over others, control and dominate delegated assignments destroy individual freedom and creativity and frustrate the desire to serve. The impulse to control others must be beaten back at every opportunity. People who are given responsibility must be allowed to carry it out.

Micro-managers are primarily concerned with themselves and their own reputations, not those of the team. These destructive tendencies often arise from feelings of inadequacy and insecurity about their own position and skills. They tend to rely too much on procedures and rules because they fear others and don't trust them. Micro-managers suck all the creativity, risk-taking, and entrepreneurial spirit out of the team. They are afraid of imagination, risk-taking, and progress.

Real trust is exhibited not when everyone agrees with the opinion of the leader but when the team stands contrary to him. When the servant leader bows his will to the wisdom of the group, valuing their wisdom, motives, and experience, he demonstrates trust. To the new leader, this feels like a cliff-jumping exercise. To the experienced team, this is a place of safety. It was for this very purpose that the team was formed and has great value. When their wisdom stands contrary to the leader's, the servant leader has to smile. This is a team assured of its role and confident in its abilities. This is the place where the true leader nods and says, "Well done. Go for it." And the higher the stakes, the greater the joy. Steve Jobs famously said, "We don't hire smart people and tell them what to do. We hire smart people and let them tell us what to do."

Chapter Eight
Love always hopes.

Leaders must have hope and convey it clearly and often to the team. Hope is not wishing something was so; rather, it is a confident expectation that it is so. Leaders are not blind. They see everything: the good, bad, and the ugly. Hope sees what is possible. Hope does not say, "I sure wish this could be done." Hope says, "It is done." Hope has strength, vision, courage, and the creativity to accomplish the impossible. And, indeed, nothing is impossible for this team. And nothing less is worthy of their time and talents. The leader is not boastful but confident in his expectation of the outcome. That is hope. All true leaders have it and need to share it with the team.

Hope never fades away, and it always inspires. The challenge for the leader is to dream big. For a vision to be inspiring, hope must fix itself on something worthy of the talents of the team. Weak leaders cast small visions, but strong leaders cast big visions that are impossible to achieve alone. The whole team is necessary to accomplish the goal. And true leaders exude confident expectation within the group, thereby encouraging them to undertake and endure.

Hope requires clear vision. It is within every leader's grasp to see and communicate a clear vision for the team, business, or enterprise, and it must be done. Hope is a light that illuminates the possible. Shared hope energizes and engages the team. Teams rally around vision.

For some reason, we have confused PowerPoint decks with vision. Numbers and graphs and clip art are not enough. It's like junk food. It tastes sweet, but it does nothing good for you. Real vision conveys truth, including facts and figures, of course. But it also conveys dreams of what is possible. Hope plants a flag on the field of the impossible, around which the team can rally. It inspires people with a cause greater than themselves. It requires more energy, more resources, and more wherewithal than any one person is capable of alone. Therein lies the excitement.

Leaders know that only big dreams inspire people. If the vision is already manageable, who needs faith, inspiration, or the team? Only big dreams are worthy of a servant leader and his or her high-performance team.

I have met several leaders who had clear and compelling visions of the future. None were as persuasive and compelling as Doug Traylor, owner of VIP Holdings in Austin, Texas. When it comes to seeing new paradigms and creating new products, he is both prophet and inspired savant. He is incredibly quick at seeing future opportunities and designing products to meet those needs. More importantly, he is so personally persuaded in the rightness of his vision that he acts. He creates new things. Hope crystallizes into reality. It is an amazing thing to watch as dreams take shape and hope becomes manifest. I have rarely seen such faith in the business world. Miracles are made of this stuff.

Chapter Nine
Love always perseveres.

Energized by vision and confident expectation, true leaders know the end from the beginning. They know what the achievement of the vision means, what it looks like. And they endure through every hardship and obstacle until they achieve it. Leadership endures all things.

One of the most important qualities of the servant leader is the willingness to persevere through the difficult times. When everything is smooth sailing, even mediocre teams can function on their own. But when the storms break and water starts pouring into the boat, everyone looks to the leader to calm the winds and waves. A true leader will persevere with peace.

More than anything, the leader must protect his peace. His peace will protect his mind and heart and vision. When trouble comes, it comes with its sidekick, fear. How do we protect our peace? In other words, what do we focus on to keep our vision and faith intact? In such times, I meditate on the important things. There is a teaching that says, "Whatever things are true, noble, and just. Whatever is pure, lovely, and of a good report; if there is anything virtuous or worthy of praise, think on these things." It's easy to get bogged down in the mundane, the boring, and the distracting. I have found that thinking along those lines reorients my compass; it realigns my thinking. Maintaining a healthy internal dialogue requires that I deliberately seek out good things to dwell upon.

Neuroscientists have proven that we are what we think. We are not what we eat. We are what we believe about ourselves and what we think, say, and do. From neurogenesis to quantum physics, scientists are beginning to understand that much of our world is formed by the meditations of our hearts and words of our mouths. If we speak it and believe it, we tend to receive. That can be energizing or frightening, depending on what we think about and what comes out of our mouths.

What are we feeding our minds? What are we saying about others? What are we saying about ourselves? What kind of environment are we creating for ourselves by the words of our mouths? We eat the feast that we prepare for ourselves. And the consequences of that, for good or ill, will determine our victories and failures, our fortunes and troubles. It will also determine whether we can endure to the end.

Sir Ernest Shackleton led an expedition to explore the Antarctic in 1909. Deep into the polar ice cap, their ship, Endurance, became trapped in the ice and was eventually crushed. Under his leadership, twenty-eight men spent more than a year with little to no food, frigid temperatures, and dim hope for rescue. But they persevered. Shackleton and his officers loved those men, sacrificed for them, and undertook heroic measures on their behalf.

More than a year after they were stranded, a small party from the group made its way from the Antarctic to Cape May and got word to the mainland. Defying death and impossible odds, they emerged intact, all saved (the world had thought them dead). Perseverance, vision, courage, hard work, and hope were the essential ingredients. Captain Shackleton and his men had an unshakable expectation of survival and rescue and persevered until it was accomplished.

My son, David, bought a failed government chicken farm in Mekelle, Ethiopia in 2010. Soon after he started operations, things began to go wrong. The water supply suddenly became saline and was unsuitable for the chickens. Someone poisoned the feed. An electrical fire threatened the coops. Then, disease attacked and threatened to wipe out the entire flock of laying hens. As a twenty-five-year-old from the suburbs, Dave knew very little about raising chickens. He felt like he was in over his head with no rescue in sight.

But he had vision, courage, and perseverance. He would not be deterred. Through sheer persistence and courage, he met every challenge and overcame them. In a relatively short time, his company emerged as the largest egg-producing enterprise in the country. Perseverance got him through. And when a leader navigates those shoals, the team gains confidence and begins to believe that nothing is impossible.

Not all of us are called to be entrepreneurs, but we can all choose to have faith. A shared vision buttressed by hope and executed with perseverance is virtually unstoppable.

Chapter Ten
Specific Warnings

There are eight characteristics against which leaders are warned:

> *"Love does not envy, it does not boast, it is not proud. It does not dishonor others, it is not self-seeking, it is not easily angered, it keeps no record of wrongs. Love does not delight in evil."*

Ordinarily, one might not take the time to list specific negative characteristics. However, the author of the text did exactly that. There is no sense in mincing words. If there are specific dangers to avoid, let's have them. For the honest, self-evaluating leader, there is as much to be gained in knowing what to avoid as there is in what to emulate.

Sad to say, I suspect most people who read through this list of behaviors will recognize a manager or two in their lives. I know I do. We are all likely to know such people and even, perhaps, work for them. That is not in question. The challenge is, how will we respond to them? How will we choose to act when under their purview? The answer lies in the first seven powerful characteristics that we have already discussed. Those are not only a list of behaviors useful for leading others, but they also help us in difficult situations.

For instance, we can always walk in grace and forgiveness. It may not make our terrible boss better, but it makes us better. And it encourages the team that labors under the negative repercussions of lousy management.

Most importantly, this list represents a clear warning to servant leaders. We must always be checking our own hearts, examining our own leadership skills, lest we fall into one of these traps. They are so insidious, they merit special attention.

Love does not envy.

The root word for "envy" is the Greek word *zelos*, which describes a person "who is radically consumed with his own desires and plans." This describes someone so bent on getting his or her own way that nothing and no one can get in the way. He or she looks upon the success of someone else and says, "That should be me, that is mine." Of course, there are less dramatic forms of envy. That slight nudge of jealousy when a colleague is rewarded, instead of us. Or the person singled out for praise at the big meeting even though you were also on the project.

An envious leader is a jealous one, one that desires recognition, advantage, or the riches of others. In business, it is imperative not to attach our affections to the wrong things. Envy says, "He did not earn that. She is not entitled to that. They don't warrant that attention, success, or reputation. I do." Envy seeks that which is not its own and fastens itself upon that which belongs to another. It is covetousness and a first cousin to theft. The envious plot, once hatched, breeds the opportunity and means to achieve its villainous purpose.

We must be vigilant to step on the snake of envy in our lives. It creeps in, unawares. It is that same spirit that tells us that we are the center of the universe, that we matter more than anyone else. It is a sneaky lie that conspires to consume our hearts and wreck our lives.

We must guard our hearts against seeking anything that is not ours, even good things. If we are careful to guard against envy, we will find opportunities for advancement and success abounding. There is no limit to what we can accomplish because motives matter. The condition of our hearts is critically important. And envy can very quickly sidetrack our otherwise good pursuits. It can be a stumbling block even to the good leader. Money itself is not evil, for example. But envy of other people's riches and the love of money are.

A rich young man, looking for the answers to his deepest questions, sought out Jesus, who loved the guy. They spoke for a while, and Jesus was so taken with him that He invited the man to join the team. However, Jesus said he would have to sell his stuff and donate it to the poor. Why? Not because having things was bad but because Jesus wanted to reveal to him that love for his riches had seized control of his heart. He turned down the offer. His stuff meant more to him than Jesus did. He walked away empty and sad. The love of money cost that man everything, including his happiness.

Love does not boast.

The origin of the word "boastful: comes from the Greek word *perperuomai*, which means "a lot of self-talk." It describes a person so full of himself that he has become his own favorite topic of conversation. Nothing and no one else matter quite as much as he does. He endlessly promotes himself and exaggerates his amazing qualities.

We live and work in a culture of self-promotion, boasting, and prideful behavior. It has risen to a level that can only be described as demonic. Seemingly gone are the popular virtues of humility and modesty. Yet the principles of leadership are timeless; they are not momentary or subject to the whims and demands of popular culture. Nonetheless, there is a truth that is superior to every societal norm and trend. Truth, being eternal in nature, stands the test of time.

Boastfulness and self-promotion and self-pride are ugly. Yet, our corporate headquarters and sales forces are full of it. Vanity is a fleeting, poisonous attribute. It is fraudulent to think that we are in any way responsible for our own success. More times than not, the contributions of others are equal to or superior to our own. And in all cases, whatever success we might enjoy is from the providential hand upon our lives and not of us. Yet, it is a common affliction of mankind. We would take credit for even our own salvation (spiritually) if we could.

A true leader is so strong, so sure, so confident, that he doesn't need to speak of himself. True leadership never vaunts itself in such a way. Remember, servant leadership always upholds the needs of the group first and himself or herself last.

As the Son of God, Jesus had every right to exalt himself, but He did not. Time after time, though the lawyers tried to bait Him, He refused to brag or boast. He set aside His privilege and titles when he began His mission on earth. He made Himself a man, tempted at all points, but obedient to His Father who sent Him. If anyone deserved to boast, it was Jesus. He was with God at the beginning. He is the King of Kings, Lord of Lords, and the Prince of Peace. Royalty runs His veins. And that doesn't even begin to include status for the miracles He did and the lives He changed. But he refused to boast. Instead, He humbled Himself and took the blows, even as they tried to kill Him.

True leaders refuse to brag or boast. They leave the selfies to others. The team always gets the credit and the glory.

Love is not proud.

The word pride means "puffed-up, swollen, or inflated with self-importance." People who carry around an air of superiority are snobbish and prideful. In the context of the Judeo-Christian life, pride has a significant place as the birthplace of original sin. The angel, Lucifer, considered himself to be equal with God. He allowed himself to be lifted up, elevated, to a place higher than it ought to have been. That evil was his downfall. But it wasn't confined to the heavenly realm. Pride has afflicted all of mankind. No one is exempt from its deception.

In a leader, the presence of pride is a telltale sign of an imminent fall. It always leads in the same direction: downward to defeat and despair. It never fails. This spirit strives and struts, puffing itself up. Pride is very impressed with its accomplishments and unconcerned about the empty room it plays to.

In our culture, self-pride is not only tolerated, it is encouraged. Groups and individuals alike are encouraged to parade themselves before others. Without a moral compass, or core values, or truth, what makes one set of behavior "better" than another? If all conduct is acceptable, who is to say what is right or wrong? The law becomes malleable, shifting with the appetites of its most vocal advocates. The mass media puts a bullhorn to the mouths of chaotic forces, and the next thing we see is a movement arising out of chaos.

Pride reads its own press clippings. It is dismissive of others. Conceit believes that it alone has the best grasp of everything important. No one else on earth could possibly have anything of significance to say. Pride is dismissive, detached, and self-reliant. Pride delights in the spotlight and applause.

The doorways of the prideful person's life are never wide enough to accommodate more than one. The team suffers from neglect and starvation under such self-absorbed leadership. In pride, we also see the emergence of selfishness, narcissism, and self-centeredness. They become celebrated traits. And the victims are civility, community, and charity. Such is the legacy of the post-truth culture.

Love does not dishonor others.

The Greek word used for "dishonor" is *aschemoneo*, which describes someone who is tactless or thoughtless. It also describes someone who is inconsiderate of others, rude, or discourteous. Their language tends to be harsh and foul. We have all heard the rudeness of someone cursing loudly, using profane and foul language, regardless of who else is in earshot. This is a person who just acts ugly.

Like its cousin, arrogance, rudeness is self-absorbed and self-important. It has teeth and seeks to bite others. It attacks and diminishes those who don't measure up to its vaunted self-importance. Rudeness behaves without regard for the welfare of others in any way. It struts on a narrow path of self-righteousness. Rudeness is acting evilly toward others. Civility requires an honoring of others, a stepping aside for the benefit of others. Rudeness spits in the eye of graciousness.

Love is not self-seeking.

The most common leadership failure is the self-seeking spirit. It insists on having its own way, its own glory. It is aggressively self-focused. It manipulates others to achieve its schemes. The selfish person will do anything to get their way, including being dishonest, treacherous, and outright lying. There are no depths to which the selfish manipulator will not go to achieve his or her ends. And the ends always justify the means.

Nearly everyone battles an impulse toward selfishness. It is innate within us. Children don't have to be taught it; it develops naturally. Even toddlers learn to say "me" and "mine" early on. Selfishness comes naturally to the human condition.

Selfish people can be very religious; their God is themselves. They place themselves and their self-importance on the very throne of their hearts, and nothing can dislodge them from that holy perch. Selfishness is a character flaw that runs deep and is difficult to remedy. Teamwork is not part of the selfish person's plan because the whole world revolves around them.

Love is not easily angered.

A first cousin to self-serving is the spirit of touchiness. It is easily offended and quick to anger. So many self-described leaders have a quick temper and are explosive in their outrage. The slightest things set them off, and they have no patience or kindness or understanding. Indeed, they seem allergic to all three. Touchy people can be set off by any trivial issue and then explode into red-faced anger. This unseemly behavior is easily provoked and hard to live with.

How easily many of us are offended. At a mere slight, we become deeply offended. How many long friendships end over slight offense? Whether they deserve it or not, we can extend forgiveness to others. If we aspire to become the best leaders possible, we must practice forgiveness. A servant leader is a forgiving leader.

Everyone has been hurt, offended, or abused at one time or another. Perhaps it happened a long time ago, or perhaps the wound is still fresh. In any case, our attitude toward that offending person is having a profound effect on us. Not them, us. When we are bruised and hurt by the conflict of our relationships and the violence of our lives, how do we respond? What can we do to heal our afflictions?

Forgive everyone in our lives.

When we do forgive someone, it's usually not them who is changed. They may not even be aware of being forgiven. And it doesn't change the offense—what happened, happened. So, who does it change? It changes us.

Once we decide to forgive, it is profoundly simple. We just do it. We deliberately decide in our hearts and minds to release that person from the debt they owe us, from the hurt they caused. Forgiveness is instant.

Forgiveness is an act of grace, not a process. It is immediate and powerful and effective on every level. It doesn't take a committee or a prayer chain or a multi-step program. It is a decision that each of us makes of our own will. In the simplest terms, forgiveness is the release of a claim against someone else. It's a transaction, sure, but its power reaches the uttermost depths, releasing our hearts from bitterness, anger, and malice.

Here's how it works: when we forgive others, it changes us; it changes our hearts. And in that moment, we are healed physically, emotionally, and spiritually. Forgiveness is a paradox; when we release others, we free ourselves.

When we forgive, the healing effects begin immediately. We feel relieved, like the weight of the world has lifted off our shoulders. Our brains begin flooding our bodies with hormones that counteract the poison of bitterness we have built up inside of us. Our spirits are lighter, freer, restored anew.

Science is demonstrating what we have known by faith: that there is deep healing in forgiveness. Researchers tell us that the moment we forgive one another, our bodies begin to release serotonin, dopamine, and oxytocin into our bloodstreams. These hormones make us feel relaxed, relieved, and at peace. Serotonin goes to work immediately, relaxing our muscles and improving our blood flow. Our stress levels decrease, and suddenly, our lungs are able to breathe deeply. As those stress levels decrease, our blood pressure and heart rate decrease, and our minds begin to relax. Dopamine floods our brains with feelings of euphoria and well-being.

I understand that simply forgiving others for what they have done seems unfair. After all, damage was done, and we've been hurt. We don't want to forgive the other person. We want justice or vengeance. If we've been hurt, getting even seems fair. And it feels a lot better than saying, "Oh, I forgive him." After all, forgiveness is not fairness. The other guy hurt us, after all. How about some justice? How about some fairness? Forgiveness is not about justice. It's about healing and peace and wholeness.

Love keeps no record of wrongs.

The servant leader keeps no record of wrongs. This is a stretch for some leaders. After all, there must be accountability. What would the HR departments say?

The nature of love and leadership insists that grace, mercy, and forgiveness are the primary tools for dealing with other people. For a high-performing team to function, there must be grace to operate without fear of reprisal for taking risks. If a poor choice is made, mercy requires a second and third and forty-ninth chance. Forgiveness is the only constant. The operating attitude must be that "everybody gets a fair shake" and that mistakes are permitted. It is the only pathway to success. In that context, the idea of someone with a clipboard keeping score of every mistake or flaw is absurd.

However, repeated poor performance, lack of effort, or substandard behavior have consequences. I have found that I have hired people into positions for which they have been a poor fit. The longer I kept them in that mismatched role, the more damage I did to both the team and the individual. If I hired the wrong person for the job, the best thing for all concerned is to remove that person at the earliest opportunity. If possible, help them find a position for which they are better-suited. But the leader is not doing that individual any favors by keeping them in the wrong position in an underperforming capacity.

Minimum standards (my friend Bob doesn't have goals, he has "minimum standards") must be maintained for the good of the team and the company. Fair evaluations are part of the deal. Everyone must be held responsible and accountable. But all of this is done in a climate of grace. And that makes all the difference.

Love does not delight in evil.

This attitude delights in fault-finding and rejoices in evil. There is no mercy in this spirit; it is just plain mean. It delights in hearing that harm or disaster has hurt people. It can't wait for the bad report on someone. Such behavior stops teamwork instantly. No one wants to work with this person, and all creativity, discovery, and inspiration is stifled. What kind of person is overjoyed when injustice is done to someone else.

This malicious spirit deliberately, calculatingly, and cooly seeks to hurt others. It keeps record of every offense and plots for the opportunity to get even. It is remorseless and relentless in tearing down others' reputations, even lying and falsifying the truth to attack them.

There is an enemy of our souls. He comes to kill, steal, and destroy. His nature is to control and power over other people. He is a liar and murderer and has been from the very start. He rejoices in evil, destruction, and death.

There is no place in the ranks of leadership for the purely selfish. They operate against the best interests of the team and the company. People who are so self-absorbed and self-involved adversely affect everyone and are a danger to the enterprise. As Bob Klein says, "On the field of battle, these people will get you killed." My counsel is to terminate them from your team as quickly as possible before they can cause too much damage.

Chapter Eleven
Love never fails.

The Greek word for "fail" is *pipto*, which means to fall from a high position or a warrior felled in battle. It is commonly used to mean "disappointment" or "ruin."

Love is the highest standard for human behavior. To the extent that true leadership adheres to this standard, it never fails. The leader may go through trouble and challenges, but it is impossible to fail. In love, the servant leader taps into a source of authority and power greater than him or herself. It is simply impossible for anyone to come out from under that power unmoved, untouched, and unchanged by the encounter.

Let me say this another way: if servant leadership is about loving and serving others, the only way to fail is by not doing it. Every time we love others, we succeed. There is always victory in love.

Personal Statement
The Highest Standard

Jesus Christ is the greatest leader of all time.

His life defined the essential elements of true leadership. In Him, we see how to inspire, motivate, and serve others. He modeled the giving, serving, unselfish nature of a servant who would change the world for all time.

Like so many truths, servant leadership is a paradox. It turns the contemporary notions of what it means to be a leader upside down. Jesus taught that the greatest leader is the greatest servant. Only by serving others do we earn the right to lead them.

Near the end of His ministry on earth, He entered Jerusalem to the sound of triumphant cheers and shouts of adoration from the pressing crowds thronging the streets. Shouts of recognition and adulation thundered throughout the city. His reputation as a miracle-making prophet, messiah, and king preceded Him. But Jesus' response was not to accept the praise of crowds. He led his twelve followers to a quiet room, grabbed a towel, and washed their dirty feet, one by one. It was an act of humble service, an act of a lowly servant, an act of love. It was the quintessential act of the servant leader.

Jesus refused the honor of men, the title of king, the adulation of the crowds. He set aside His rights and nobility so that others could approach Him, talk with Him, and walk with Him. Why? So that the Son could reveal the Father. For centuries, God had been regarded as a far-off God, unapproachable and unavailable to mortal man. All of that changed with Jesus. He delighted in engaging people, hearing their problems, healing, teaching, loving them and, through it all, pointing to the goodness of the Father Himself!

Jesus agreed to become a sacrificial lamb to satisfy judgment meant for us. He didn't die as a king; He died as a servant. But this was no ordinary servant. He forsook a crown to be nailed to a cross. He gave up all honor and standing to deny Himself for our sake. He endured the shame instead of the applause. He welcomed pain instead of riches and ease. He suffered and died so that we might live and serve each other. It cost Him everything.

To contemplate the price that was paid by Jesus, the Son of God, who came to serve as Son of man causes a hushed silence to overwhelm our souls. It causes us to barely breathe at the horror and honor of it all. The moment dares us not to speak, lest it offend the Son. It is a holy moment in our souls and spirits.

There is only one "perfect leader" because there was only one perfect servant. He paid a price that no one else could pay to purchase a destiny no one else could afford. And He did it for all time: past, present, and future. He paid it once and for all, that we might enter a new paradigm, a new strategic plan from God. And it is the nature of that plan for us to succeed and prosper and bless others. It is the design of that plan to provide for all our needs and desires forever. The Father sits above the whole earth, watching over His plan, providing every resource to ensure its success.

We are that plan. Our businesses are included in His grand design. In fact, it is our industry and creativity and drive that enables what He desires for mankind. By serving others, we fulfill that design. In service to our employees and customers, we emulate the Servant. He releases all the provisions of heaven to us who believe. There is no better strategic plan than His.

So, what does all this mean to us? How then shall we lead? The elements of servanthood, of true leadership, are the elements of love. They are profound, powerful, and eternal. They are empowered by God and never fail to achieve their strategic and tactical goals. The elements of servanthood always fulfill their destiny. Why? Because they are conceived, ordained, and empowered by God.

There is no greater love than one who lays down his life for his friends. In a manner of speaking, this is the call of leadership. To sacrifice freely of ourselves for the sake of the team; to accept the responsibilities (and blame) and give others the credit; to regard the needs of our followers higher than our own. There is no higher standard. There is no greater example than Jesus Himself. He died so that everyone on earth could freely choose their destinies.

What did it cost Jesus to be the perfect example of a servant leader? It cost Him everything. What will it cost us? It could cost time and fame and self-promotion. The price is humility and giving of ourselves to others. What is our reward? The reward is the satisfaction of a being a leader engaged in an enterprise so much greater than him or herself. And, then, there's eternity.

For more information, please visit us at **www.jeffellis.us.**

Endnotes

Chapter One

"He who is greatest among you shall be your servant." Matthew
    23:11. NKJV.

"People who are out to prove something…"
Vanier, Jean. (1989). *Community and Growth: Authority as a Gift*. p. 214.
Paulist Press: Mahwah, New Jersey.

"Inside each of us is a little tyrant…" Ibid. p. 216

"interfere in the work of others…" Ibid. p. 216.

"help the growth and freedom of individuals." Ibid. p. 209.

"Human beings grow best in a relaxed environment…" Ibid. p. 215

Chapter Two

"But the servant leader's goal…"
Vanier, Jean. (1989). *Community and Growth: Authority as a Gift*. p. 212.
Paulist Press: Mahwah, New Jersey.

"Love is patient, love is kind…" 1 Corinthians 1:13.
    NIV.

Chapter Three

"makrothumia." p. 671.
Renner, Rick. (2003). *Sparkling Gems from the Greek I*. p. 671
Harrison House: Tulsa, OK.

"…candle with a very long wick." Ibid. p. 671

"…monopoly on insights and gifts;…"
Vanier, Jean. (1989). *Community and Growth: Authority as a Gift*. p. 205.
Paulist Press: Mahwah, New Jersey.

Myers Briggs Assessment: MBTI®
Retrieved from: www.myersbriggs.org

Chapter Four

"…please help my unbelief." Mark 9:24.
    KJV.
Wooden, John, & Jamison, Steve. (1997). *Wooden: A Lifetime of
    Observations and Reflection On and Off the Court*.
Contemporary Books: Lincolnwood, IL

Chapter Five

"Search my heart and see if there is anything here…" Psalm 139:23.
    NKJV.

Citizens United vs Federal Election commission (2010).
Holding: Political spending is a form of protected speech under
    the First Amendment, and the government may not keep
    corporations or unions from spending money to support or
    denounce individual candidates in elections.

Retrieved from:www.scotusblog.com/case-files/cases/citizens-
    united-v-federal-election-commission

Chapter Six

…stego,… ." p. 684.
Renner, Rick. (2003). *Sparkling Gems from the Greek I*. p. 671
Harrison House: Tulsa, OK.

"There was a woman, famously caught in adultery…" John 8:4.
    NKJV.

Chapter Nine

Worsley, Captain F.A. (1931). *Endurance: An Epic of Polar Adventure.* W. W. Norton & Co.: New York, NY.

Chapter Ten

"Love does not envy, it does not boast…" 1 Corinthians 13. NKJV.

…*zelos*…" p. 672.
Renner, Rick. (2003). *Sparkling Gems from the Greek I.* Harrison House: Tulsa, OK.

"A rich young man, looking for answers…" Luke 18:18. NKJV.

…*perperuomai*…" p. 674.
Renner, Rick. (2003). *Sparkling Gems from the Greek I.* Harrison House: Tulsa, OK.

…*aschemoneo*…" p. 676.
Renner, Rick. (2003). *Sparkling Gems from the Greek I.* Harrison House: Tulsa, OK.

Chapter Eleven

"…*pipto*…..." p. 687.
Renner, Rick. (2003). *Sparkling Gems from the Greek I.* Harrison House: Tulsa, OK.

CPSIA information can be obtained
at www.ICGtesting.com
Printed in the USA
LVHW091036071118
595662LV00003B/125/P

9 781732 609624